DIVISION, INTOLERANCE, AND CONFLICT

Can Public Civility Ever Be Restored?

Stuart A. Kallen

ReferencePoint
Press

San Diego, CA

About the Author

Stuart A. Kallen is the author of more than 350 nonfiction books for children and young adults. He has written on topics ranging from the theory of relativity to the art of electronic dance music. In 2018 Kallen won a Green Earth Book Award from the Nature Generation environmental organization for his book *Trashing the Planet: Examining the Global Garbage Glut*. In his spare time he is a singer, songwriter, and guitarist in San Diego.

Picture Credits:
Cover: pathdoc/Shutterstock Images

6: mariyaermolaeva/Shutterstock Images
10: kryzhov/Shutterstock Images
12: Associated Press
15: Hayk_Shalunts/Shutterstock Images
18: fizkes/Shutterstock Images
20: Tada Images/Shutterstock Images
23: Sipa USA/Associated Press

27: Featureflash Photo Agency/Shutterstock
29: MediaPunch Inc/Alamy Stock Photo
35: SOPA Images Limited/Alamy Stock Photo
39: Omeer/Shutterstock Images
42: Jerel Cooper/Shutterstock Images
44: David Bokuchava/Shutterstock Images
50: as-artmedia/Shutterstock Images
52: Associated Press
54: Reuters/Alamy Stock Photo

LIBRARY OF CONGRESS CATALOGING-IN-PUBLICATION DATA

Names: Kallen, Stuart A., author.
Title: Division, Intolerance, and Conflict : Can public civility ever be restored?/ by Stuart A. Kallen.
Description: San Diego, CA : Reference Point Press, Inc., 2023.
| Includes bibliographical references
and index.
Identifiers: 2022015292 | ISBN 9781678203306 (library binding) |
ISBN 9781678203313 (ebook)
Subjects: LCSH: United States. violence--Juvenile literature. | Mental
health services--United States--Juvenile literature.
Media literacy--Juvenile literature.

Contents

Introduction   4
The Anger Pandemic

Chapter One   8
What Is Civility, and Why Does It Matter?

Chapter Two   17
Americans Behaving Badly

Chapter Three   26
Cable News and Social Media Instigators

Chapter Four   37
The Increasingly Ugly World of Politics

Chapter Five   48
Stepping Back from Anger

Source Notes   57
For Further Research   60
Index   62

The Anger Pandemic

Almost everyone has seen the videos: brawls in restaurants, red-faced citizens screaming at school officials, and passengers on airplanes throwing punches at flight attendants. It seems as if one side-effect of the 2020 COVID-19 pandemic was a plague of widespread, uncontrollable anger. And that might be true. Psychology professor Raymond Novaco, who specializes in anger assessment and treatment, calls the pandemic "a big anger incubator."[1] Novaco says the isolation, fear, and uncertainty caused by the pandemic left people feeling frustrated, anxious, and helpless as the world seemed to spin out of control. Stressful feelings like these are commonly expressed in outbursts of anger.

Much of the rage was initially directed at workers required to enforce government mask mandates. While the mandates helped slow the spread of COVID-19, those who did not wish to wear masks screamed in anger at employees in restaurants and stores. Some workers were physically assaulted when asking patrons to wear a mask. The problem was particularly bad for flight attendants, who had to deal with unruly passengers upset over mask mandates. Flight attendant Adam Mosley expressed his frustration: "It's mentally exhausting to have to police adults over this matter. . . . [But] there is definitely a subset of people that don't seem to think that any of the rules apply to them."[2]

The rules of civility that govern behavior in public were also tested by other issues related to the pandemic. A record number of employees quit their jobs for various reasons, including the inability to arrange child care and fear of contract-

ing the disease. This resulted in staff shortages, empty shelves in stores and supermarkets, and higher prices everywhere. Customers affected by these problems tended to take out their anger and frustration on employees, the nearest target. Annabelle Cardona, who works at a home-improvement store in Massachusetts, says she deals with out-of-control customers all the time. The screaming used to make her weep, but no longer. "I've been calloused by it," she says. "Now, instead of crying, I'm just really pessimistic and judgmental against the people around me."[3]

The pandemic is not entirely to blame for bad behavior. People seem to have been getting more emotional for years, and many blame the media. There are entire industries that profit by stoking division, intolerance, and conflict. Some of the most popular podcasts, radio talk shows, and cable news programs keep viewers amped up and angry. Hosts of these shows spew incendiary language to blame minorities, immigrants, and political opponents for the ills of the nation. Those who hold different political or ethical beliefs are described as vile, unpatriotic, un-American, and even treasonous. This has led to a spike in threats and actual physical violence directed at politicians, poll workers, teachers, health care workers, scientists, and others.

Bad for the Body

Mental health professionals have long known that unmanaged anger can turn into aggression. Often the targets of that aggression are spouses, siblings, and friends. But within the social sphere, millions direct their anger at those who look, think, or act differently from them. And unchecked rage is bad not only for victims but also for those who live with a mix of toxic emotions. Being angry

all the time triggers negative health effects, including insomnia, depression, high blood pressure, stroke, and heart attack.

It does not have to be this way. Studies suggest that there are links between heavy use of social media and negative emotions. "Disaster television viewing"—obsessively viewing news programs after natural- and human-caused disasters—can increase negative emotions, leading to angry outbursts, irritability, and aggression. Psychiatrist Joshua Morganstein suggests ways to avoid anger-induced problems. "We all have to be very cautious with our exposures to the media," he says. "There is so much stimulation and so much information. And much of it is not good news. . . . We really could all stand more media breaks."[4]

Despite the divisive news, an overwhelming majority of people care about their neighbors and are polite to one another. They make a point of thanking flight attendants, tipping restaurant workers, and leaving good reviews for service workers. And most respond with kindness when bad things happen to others. In 2020 alone, Americans donated a record $471 billion to charity.

Unpleasant people get a lot of attention, thanks to viral videos and clickbait news stories. But those who learn to focus on the positive often feel better and just might live longer. Morganstein says that people need to spend "more time walking outside, seeing our neighbors, saying hello, exchanging problem-solving [ideas], and reminding each other that we're in this together."[5]

What Is Civility, and Why Does It Matter?

Talk of incivility is everywhere. Judging by the number of current articles on the subject, the loss of civility seems like a new problem. But incivility has been a topic of concern in the United States since the country's inception. George Washington, for example, wrote an essay called *Rules of Civility and Decent Behaviour in Company and Conversation* in 1744 to define how a respectable person in the new nation should act. Etiquette guides remained in fashion for decades as incivility seemed to be threatened by influxes of immigrants in urban centers, the growth of an industrial working class, and even the rising independence of women. In the modern era, discussions of public rudeness and vulgarity center on politics, talk radio, cable news, rap music, video games, violent movies, social media, and the COVID-19 pandemic.

While almost everyone seems to think that rudeness is rising to ever higher levels in the twenty-first century, not everyone agrees on what constitutes civility or its decline. For Washington, it was a list of maxims on how to behave "in company and conversation." Today, though, some see the loss of civility through the political lens of two opposing sides insulting each other as they squabble over issues. Others view incivility as the lack of politeness in public. They curse, push to the front of the line, lay on their car horns, insult strangers, and yell at restaurant servers and cashiers. While some wish angry people would just be more polite, author ZZ Packer does not think this will solve problems associated with incivility. She maintains, "The obvious kind of civility, the civility of niceness, is only the most superficial marker of much deeper moral obligations."[6]

> "The obvious kind of civility, the civility of niceness, is only the most superficial marker of much deeper moral obligations."[6]
>
> —ZZ Packer, novelist

Enlightened Thinkers

The term *civility* evolved from Latin. It denotes the responsibility of being a good citizen. In this usage, *civility* includes principles like politeness, respect, and empathy for others. The Greek philosopher Aristotle used the term *civil society* to describe citizens who share ethical standards and morals. In a civil society people could live freely and safely under a common rule of law. In the seventeenth century, English philosopher Thomas Hobbes expanded on the concept of civil society in his groundbreaking political tract *Leviathan*. Hobbes linked civility with an idea called the social contract, a term still in use today. Citizens who are part of the social contract agree to surrender some of their more corrupt impulses, such as greed, aggression, and revenge, for peace and order under a central government. Hobbes wrote that without a social contract, humanity would descend into chaos and total war, making life "solitary, poor, nasty, brutish, and short."[7]

The social contract theory was a major inspiration to the founders of the United States. The Constitution starts with the words "We the people." This simple phrase expresses the ideas embodied in the social contract; it is the people who are giving their mutual consent to be governed. In exchange for this consent, the social contract requires governing authorities to keep the peace while granting people certain rights, such as free speech and freedom of religion.

Packer links the social contract spelled out in the Constitution to what she calls the moral and political duty of civility. "We must operate in good faith . . . offer fair terms of cooperation, fashion rational arguments for our positions and depend, in the absence of agreement, on mutual consent," she says. "We must behave as though everyone shares a common stake in the flourishing of the civic whole."[8]

Order or Justice?

Some might see cooperation and consent as necessary for society to function smoothly, even when there are strong disagreements. But calls for civility have long been used to stifle political protest. Civil rights activist Martin Luther King Jr. addressed this problem in 1963. While King was in jail for taking part in nonviolent protests against Alabama's racist segregation policies, he wrote "Letter from a Birmingham Jail." The open letter was not addressed to violent racists in the Ku Klux Klan but instead to local White clergy members who argued in favor of civility over rowdy street demonstrations. The White leaders often said that Black

Some people say that incivility is a lack of politeness in public, such as when drivers honk their horns or yell at pedestrians or other drivers.

Civil Disobedience and the Civil Rights Act

In the early 1960s the civil rights movement was harshly criticized by some for using nonviolent tactics like sit-ins and street marches. But the movement, led by Martin Luther King Jr., was successful despite those aligned against it. Congress passed the Civil Rights Act of 1964, which outlawed discrimination in public places such as restaurants, bus stations, and motels. The Voting Rights Act, passed in 1965, guaranteed the right to vote to all Americans whatever their race. These acts swept away nearly a century of racist laws that prevented Black Americans from exercising their civil rights.

King was central to the passage of those landmark bills. President Lyndon B. Johnson met with King regularly to work for passage of the legislation. While the two men often had a tense relationship, they worked together in a civil manner that helped them succeed against fierce opposition from southern senators. While systemic racism did not end, the laws stand as a testament to civil disobedience as a means for changing civil society.

people should not march in the streets to advocate for civil rights; rather, they should argue for equality in court and meet with local leaders to end segregation. King pointed out that civil methods like negotiating had already been tried, and they had failed.

King believed that the calls for civility from moderate Whites posed bigger problems than the actions of the Klan. He insisted, "The Negro's great stumbling block in the stride toward freedom is . . . the white moderate who is more devoted to order than to justice; who prefers a negative peace which is the absence of tension to a positive peace which is the presence of justice; who constantly says, 'I agree with you in the goal you seek, but I can't agree with your methods of direct action.'"[9]

While White leaders called for civility over justice, King and other activists used civil disobedience to achieve their goals. These protesters disobeyed unjust laws against free expression and ignored commands given by authorities to disperse. This type of disobedience is considered civil because it is nonviolent; demonstrators peacefully take to the streets to express political beliefs.

In Birmingham, Alabama, more than one thousand Black protesters ignored a court order that barred protesters from marching.

And they defied police orders to stop when they attempted to take over downtown streets while demanding equal rights. King explained his tactics in the open letter. "Nonviolent direct action seeks to create such a crisis and foster such a tension that a community which has constantly refused to negotiate is forced to confront the issue," he wrote. "It seeks so to dramatize the issue that it can no longer be ignored."[10]

Birmingham police reacted to the civil disobedience in a manner that shocked the conscience of the nation. News reports from Birmingham at that time show authorities attacking protesters—many of them children and young adults—with clubs, police dogs, and high-pressure fire hoses.

Martin Luther King Jr. gives his famous "I Have a Dream" speech in Washington, DC, in 1963. King encouraged the use of civil disobedience as a way to advance civil rights.

Outlawing Civil Disobedience

In 2020 another massive display of civil disobedience occurred after police in Minneapolis, Minnesota, killed a Black man named George Floyd during an arrest. The event, which was captured on video by a young bystander, triggered a massive wave of protests throughout the country. The demonstrations, loosely organized under the Black Lives Matter (BLM) banner, took place in every US state and spread to countries around the globe. In some places, George Floyd protesters defied authorities by using civil disobedience tactics. They marched in the streets without proper permits, camped on the grounds of state capitols, defaced monuments of Confederate Civil War figures, and blocked traffic on interstate highways. The disobedience remained largely civil, according to the Armed Conflict Location & Event Data Project (ACLED), which usually studies war zones and political upheaval in developing nations. After analyzing 7,750 BLM protests in more than 2,400 locations in all 50 states, ACLED concluded that 96 percent of the events were peaceful and nondestructive.

"Nonviolent direct action seeks to create such a crisis and foster such a tension that a community which has constantly refused to negotiate is forced to confront the issue."[10]

—Martin Luther King Jr., civil rights leader

As the BLM movement expanded over the summer of 2020, the most disruptive protesters received a disproportionate amount of attention in the media. This gave BLM opponents ammunition to portray the small percentage of people who looted and burned buildings as representative of the entire movement. In the wake of the Floyd protests, lawmakers in at least thirty-six states introduced more than ninety anti-protest bills. While rioting and arson were already illegal in all states, some of the laws target those who engage in civil disobedience. For example, after the new laws passed in Iowa, Oklahoma, Tennessee, and elsewhere, protesters could be charged with felonies

A Case Against Civility

Alex Zamalin is a director of the African American Studies Program at the University of Detroit Mercy. In his 2021 book, *Against Civility*, Zamalin explains why he opposes calls for social justice activists to be civil:

[Civility is] remarkably effective at neutralizing opposition. Saying, "Be civil" to someone expressing legitimate . . . grievances transforms the conversation. Now the supposedly uncivil person must play by the terms or be chastised; they must prove that their demands are reasonable in the first place, that they aren't being extreme. They must spend time proving that they deserve to be taken seriously, rather than articulating their demands. The preacher of civility, however, having assumed the defensive position, leaves the conversation without having to defend their own position. This is how rulers maintain a society in which inequality is the norm and injustice an incontrovertible fact; they silence opposition by disqualifying its legitimacy from the start. . . . Police, vigilante groups, racial terrorists, and prison wardens . . . are deployed to discipline citizens labeled as uncivil. . . . Politicians, lobbyists, public intellectuals, and media elites determine what constitutes civil and uncivil behavior.

Alex Zamalin, *Against Civility*. New York: Beacon, 2021, pp. 18–19.

for minor crimes like obstructing traffic, blocking sidewalks, or trespassing. Some laws seemed specifically aimed at forcing people to be nice. A Kentucky law makes it a crime to insult or taunt a police officer with offensive words or gestures. The new anti-protest laws seem to specifically target people of color. According to Omar Wasow, an assistant professor of politics at Pomona College, "These laws will be selectively employed and they will be way disproportionately used in particular against Black activists."[11]

Morals and Manners

Those who oppose anti-protest laws say they are unconstitutional because they restrict the right to free speech guaranteed by the First Amendment of the Constitution. The courts have yet to decide. Whatever the outcome in the courts, the laws are part of a trend that seeks to regulate what some see as uncivil behavior. But Alex Zamalin, director of the African American Studies Program at the University of Detroit Mercy, points out:

> Civility hasn't been the organizing principle of the most successful anti-racist thinkers . . . who have sought to dismantle U.S. racism. They discovered, over and over again, that real political change happens through direct struggle, without obligation to decorum or propriety. . . . Shocking and provoking people—no matter how impolite the words and actions might seem—is necessary to wake the majority of people from their moral slumber.[12]

Zamalin draws a distinction between manners and morals. Manners like courtesy, respect, and good conduct help society function while promoting cooperation and peaceful relations. Fighting for a

In 2020 there were large displays of civil disobedience as well as violence after police in Minneapolis killed a Black man named George Floyd during an arrest. This picture shows a protestor in Los Angeles holding a shirt with a portrait of Floyd as a police car burns behind him.

moral cause, such as equal rights, can contradict the civility of manners. Civic morals require people to reject calls for peace and politeness in the face of civil wrongs. Packer contends that creating a just society "requires us to be vigilant, finding ways to keep our civic commitments even when our opponents abandon them, refuse to play fair and act in bad faith."[13]

United and Divided

Solving complex problems in a civil society often requires compromise, even with those who do not play fair, because all public protests and street demonstrations eventually end. When the marchers return home and pack away their protest signs, a different kind of work begins. Activists need to raise money, lobby politicians, educate the public, and organize in their communities. And they might have to fight for their causes in the courts, where patience, respect, and rational debate are the rule.

The hardest work of exacting change in a civil society requires activists to seek consensus with a well-organized opposition. Those who make personal contact with adversaries can come to understand the beliefs, background, opinions, and tactics of their opponents. This knowledge might put activists in a stronger position and help them develop a plan to respond to attacks. The American Civil Liberties Union of Tennessee's *Guide for Youth Activists* explains why remaining civil with adversaries can be beneficial: "[Opponents] are more likely to fight 'fair' if the other side is not a nameless, faceless 'enemy.' Furthermore, they may be an ally on another issue in the future. Assessing where the opposition is coming from will aid you in determining the best strategy for moving forward with them, whether you negotiate a compromise or battle the issue out in a public forum."[14] This view stems from a belief that civilly engaging with the opposition is a time-honored tradition in the United States. Law professor Keith Bybee contends that "civility is the baseline of respect that we owe one another in public life."[15] Americans want to believe that this baseline is still in place during public debates.

Americans Behaving Badly

There were a lot of videos making the rounds on social media showing crazy public outbursts in 2022, but the brawl at the Golden Corral restaurant in Bensalem, Pennsylvania, in February was exceptional. The fracas began when customer Alexis Rios, who was second in the buffet line, received his steak from a chef before the patron who was first in line. Rios had ordered his steak rare, so it was finished cooking before the first customer's steak, but that individual thought it was unfair. Harsh words were exchanged, bystanders got involved, and within seconds an all-out brawl erupted. A viral video shows people pushing, shoving, throwing punches, and using tables, chairs, and even booster seats to bludgeon one another. Around forty people were involved in the melee that sent customers running for the exits as employees attempted to intervene. Fortunately, no one was seriously injured.

Rios said he believed a simple misunderstanding turned into a free-for-all because everyone was wearing masks due to COVID-19 restrictions, and communication might have been difficult. "[With] masks and everything, nobody can hear nobody sometimes. There's a lot of commotion in there, the cooks behind there are talking, nobody can hear nobody. You have to speak up loud,"[16] he insisted.

Rude Customers, Low Pay, Long Hours

While the brawl at the Golden Corral was notable for its size, the video is only one among hundreds on social media that show restaurant patrons behaving badly. Mean customers bellow at servers about mask mandates and complain about food shortages or long waits for tables. Some even assault restaurant employees when the food is not to their liking. In 2021 a woman in Temple, Texas, threw her soup in a cashier's face because it was too hot. Like Rios, those who bear the brunt of such behavior blame the pandemic. As Florida restaurant worker Mary Martin Hafiani said in 2021, "[Customers] feel like they are more entitled than they have been before. . . . Their expectations are above and beyond what was the norm. I think a lot has to do with maybe they've been inside too much. And now they're out, they're taking out their frustration on the servers a lot. It's never good enough, it's not fast enough."[17]

Cruel customer conduct pushed restaurant workers to quit in droves. There has always been a high turnover in the restaurant industry due to low pay and long hours. But a record-breaking

An angry man confronts a waitress. Rude, angry customers pushed thousands of restaurant workers to quit their jobs in 2021.

892,000 food service workers walked away from their jobs in August 2021 alone, according to the Bureau of Labor Statistics. This labor shortage increased problems for those who kept their jobs. When fewer people are cooking and serving, wait times are longer. Additionally, the number of to-go orders spiked during the pandemic, which contributed to the hostile restaurant atmosphere. Wisconsin restaurant hostess and manager Stephanie Le Mere explained, "[Our kitchen has] twice as many orders with all the takeout orders we get, so the cooks get all stressed out and then the customer's food takes longer and then the customers get mad and it's just a vicious cycle."[18] To add to her stress, Le Mere has a health condition that makes her a high risk for serious problems if she contracts COVID-19.

Mask Meltdowns

During the height of the pandemic, waitstaff often dealt with what were known as mask meltdowns. These outbursts of anger, rudeness, and sometimes violent behavior were the result of Americans who were resistant to government mandates to wear a mouth and nose covering as a safety measure to slow the spread of the virus. While the mandates varied from state to state, the rules were enforced in many places from mid-2020 through early 2022, when states, communities, and businesses had the option to forgo them as transmission decreased.

A 2020 Pew Research Center poll showed that 71 percent of Americans supported mask mandates. But despite the widespread acceptance, mask mandates quickly became a hot-button issue in America's culture wars. Opponents claimed the mandates restricted their personal freedom or falsely claimed masks were not a viable preventative. Some resisters grudgingly put on masks when asked by servers or workers in stores. But during the height of the pandemic, countless videos on social media showed people screaming, throwing things, and hurling insults at workers who had the unpleasant task of enforcing mask rules.

One viral video showed a woman trashing a mask display at a Phoenix Target store, while another captured a woman in a New York bagel shop deliberately coughing on a patron who asked her to put on a mask.

Meltdowns over masks racked up millions of hits on social media. This encouraged others to engage in bad behavior. But New York University behavioral science professor David Abrams says the videos also appeal to those who support mask mandates; mask-less people throwing temper tantrums makes mask wearers feel superior. They experience satisfaction when the mandate violators get thrown out of stores. But Abrams feels empathy for

This photo shows a Target store in Portland, Oregon. During the height of the pandemic, videos on social media showed people screaming, throwing things, and hurling insults at workers in Target and other stores.

Air Rage

In 2021 the Federal Aviation Administration (FAA) stated that there were more than 5,900 reports of unruly passengers during flights. The reports resulted in 1,116 official investigations. In 2019, before the pandemic, the agency conducted only 146 investigations of unruly passengers.

Flight attendants are trained to deal with medical emergencies, security threats, and airplane evacuations. Though they have had to deal sporadically with unruly fliers in the past, confronting nasty passengers is now a predictable part of the job. As a flight attendant named Charlotte explains, air rage is now the biggest danger she faces. "These days I come to work anticipating disruptive behavior," she says. "Our colleagues are anxious, fearful. What is going to happen on the next flight? How will this passenger react if I remind them to wear their mask? Will complying with airline policies set them off? Can I avoid engaging, or would that be an evasion of my duties?"

Passengers who act up on planes can find themselves in serious trouble. The FAA has a zero-tolerance policy for violating federal airline regulations, such as failing to obey a flight attendant. Several unruly passengers have faced fines up to $45,000, and airlines have banned some from their flights.

Quoted in Dawn Gilbertson, "'Anxious, Fearful' Flight Attendants Plead for Congress' Help to Deal with Air Rage," *USA Today*, September 21, 2021. www.usatoday.com.

those who lose their temper in public over mask mandates because they might be feeling a type of primal fear that sets off an alarm in their brain. He says:

> From a psychological point of view, when there's a massive unknown new threat [like COVID-19], humans' survival instinct triggers and they become highly vigilant and emotional. You have the rug pulled from under you, and suddenly your instinct is immediately to become hyperalert. And as that adrenaline pumps, you get into what we call the fight or flight—an emotional response that overrides cool-headed rationality.[19]

Bullying of School Officials

Mask mandates became an especially contentious issue when students in many states were required to wear masks to school beginning in September 2020. While the mandates were often instituted by state governors, members of school boards were required to oversee the details of how the mandates were enacted. School board meetings were traditionally sparsely attended affairs in which mundane matters such as budgets and staffing were discussed. After school mask mandates went into effect, meetings in dozens of places suddenly overflowed with screaming, angry people protesting the new rules. Hostility increased after COVID-19 vaccination requirements were implemented for students in some states in 2021.

Social media is full of videos showing adults at school board meetings behaving like schoolyard bullies. In Williamson County, Tennessee, a doctor who testified in favor of a districtwide school mask mandate was surrounded by a crowd of protesters as he left the meeting in his car. Protesters accused the doctor of being a child abuser while shouting, "We will find you," "We know who you are," and "There is a place in hell for you . . . and everybody's taking notes, buddy."[20]

In Loudoun County, Virginia, an August 2021 school board meeting got so rowdy that police were called to clear the room. And threats to officials continued after the meeting ended. Brenda Sheridan, a Loudoun County school board member, was mailed a letter by an anonymous source that called her vile names while threatening to kill her and her adult child. This was only one of several obscene and menacing letters, texts, and emails that Sheridan and her family received.

Combative attendees at school board meetings included local parents, adults who did not live in the school district, and even those who did not have any children. Vladimir Kogan, a professor of political science at Ohio State University, contended, "These are really adult battles over adult partisanship, and the interest of kids is of secondary importance to them."[21]

People at a 2021 school board meeting in Viera, Florida, demonstrate against mandatory face masks in school. School mask mandates during the pandemic led to angry protests at school board meetings around the United States.

The Government Responds

Sheridan's experiences were not unique. In 2022 the news agency Reuters interviewed thirty-three school board members across fifteen states. These officials reported receiving 220 threatening and harassing messages. Board members have been accused of committing treason or brainwashing children. Harassing messages included threats of violence and sexual assault, as well as expressions of racism, anti-Semitism, and homophobia. In fifteen counties examined by Reuters, school officials or parents considered the threats serious enough to report them to the police or the Federal Bureau of Investigation (FBI). Most threats were sent anonymously by people using fake email addresses or other techniques to hide their identity. But Reuters was able to trace some of the messages to people who lived out of state or had no connection to the school district. As Sheridan states, "There's no way to know: Did that come from someone from another state, or is it my neighbor down the street who knows my routine?"[22]

School board members are often unpaid volunteers, and many have turned in their resignation over the harassment. Others are

The US Department of Justice Acts

Local authorities rarely have the time or expertise to track down anonymous threats to school board officials. But the problem was so severe by October 2021 that the National School Boards Association (NSBA) asked the US Department of Justice to step in. The NSBA, a nonprofit that represents over ninety thousand school board members, sent a letter to Attorney General Merrick Garland listing numerous shocking incidents directed at school officials in California, Florida, Michigan, Ohio, Wisconsin, and elsewhere.

Garland announced that the FBI would consult with federal, state, and local authorities to address the problem. As Garland wrote in a press release, "Those who dedicate their time and energy to ensuring that our children receive a proper education in a safe environment deserve to be able to do their work without fear for their safety. While spirited debate about policy matters is protected under our Constitution, that protection does not extend to threats of violence or efforts to intimidate individuals based on their views."

Merrick Garland, "Justice Department Addresses Violent Threats Against School Officials and Teachers," US Department of Justice, October 4, 2021. www.justice.gov.

living in fear after taking actions they never would have associated with their jobs. A school board member in Gwinnett County, Georgia, bought a gun for self-protection after a spate of online harassment. In Union County, North Carolina, a board member installed numerous security cameras outside her house. Sheridan says she rarely goes out alone in public anymore.

It Is Not Okay to Yell

School board meetings are local and open to the public. This makes them an easy target for those who are angry over mask mandates or some other heated cultural issue. While irate citizens might not be able to personally confront a powerful congressperson or the president, they can vent their anger at defenseless school board volunteers. And some shouting matches at school board meetings are not as spontaneous as they seem. In 2022 many protesters were egged on by an organization called Moms for Liberty, which claims to have 135 chapters with 56,000 members. The group was founded by conservative Florida activist Tina Descovich and has received funding from wealthy Republican donors. Moms for Liberty organized picket lines in front of the homes of school board members, tracked social media accounts of school officials, and swarmed school board meetings.

Many of these activists seemed alarmed that Americans were turning away from so-called traditional values promoted by conservatives. The change can be seen in polls that show young people holding more progressive views than their parents about racial issues, LGBTQ rights, and other matters. A 2020 survey taken by Tufts University found that over 25 percent of respondents aged eighteen to twenty-four had attended a BLM march or demonstration. That is up from 10 percent in 2016. Professor of education Adam Laats puts these figures in perspective: "In the face of these changes, conservative parents and activists are doing the only thing they can: disrupting their local school board meetings to make their anger felt. . . . School boards are viewed as winnable battlegrounds that activists can turn into islands of the 'real' America, in a rising sea of cultural change."[23]

While a large majority of Americans do not support turning schools, restaurants, or airplanes into political battlegrounds, some feel that they have a right to lash out when their moral convictions are threatened. This allows them to dehumanize their opponents, according to psychology professor Linda Skitka. "So if the other side is [seen as] evil, it's not a far stretch to say it's OK to yell at them,"[24] she explains. While anger might be justified in the face of serious threats, yelling at others rarely changes their views.

Most Americans believe that civil society functions best when citizens make clearheaded decisions based on facts rather than emotions. When people forget basic rules of civility, they increase stress and hostility while failing to provide positive solutions to problems that need to be solved.

Cable News and Social Media Instigators

In the early 2000s comedian Jon Stewart was riding high as the host of *The Daily Show* on Comedy Central. Stewart rose to fame making fun of cable news shows that engaged in divisive cultural wars. But when he appeared on the CNN debate show *Crossfire* in 2004, Stewart was not in the mood to tell jokes. At the time, *Crossfire* pitted liberal political operative Paul Begala against conservative pundit Tucker Carlson. Stewart criticized the *Crossfire* debate format and called the hosts partisan hacks. He said the show reduced extremely important issues to simplistic talking points that only appealed to extremists in each party. As Stewart told Carlson, "I'm here to confront you, because we need help from the media and they're hurting us. . . . It's hurting America. Here is what I wanted to tell you guys: Stop. You have a responsibility to the public discourse, and you fail miserably."[25]

Stewart's criticism of *Crossfire* sparked a widespread public debate about the role of the news media. *Crossfire*, which had been on the air since 1982, was canceled three months later. CNN president Jonathan Klein said at the time, "I agree wholeheartedly with Jon Stewart's overall premise."[26]

The Rise of Rush Limbaugh and Partisan Talk Shows

A lot has changed since Stewart was able to get a debate show canceled because it seemed to be hurting America. One major transformation is the way people consume the news. Stewart, who was born in 1962, grew up during an era when three major television networks dominated the news business. In this environment, news shows on NBC, CBS, and ABC tried to reach the widest possible audience by remaining politically neutral. A few shows featured left-versus-right political debates, but these were the exception. Most presented the news as impartially and straightforwardly as possible.

Jon Stewart is pictured at the Emmy Awards show in 2015. In 2004 Stewart was able to get a television debate show canceled after saying that it was hurting America.

News shows ran commercials but were not expected to turn a profit. Networks paid for news shows with the money generated by popular prime-time sitcoms, cop shows, medical dramas, and other programs watched by most Americans. The news was considered a prestige offering that would bring the network respect and an occasional award for outstanding coverage.

The news monopoly held by the networks and cable stations began to crack in 1988 with the rise of conservative talk radio, led by a former Top 40 disc jockey named Rush Limbaugh. Rather than focusing on objectivity, Limbaugh promoted conservative principles and badmouthed everything liberals advanced. He heightened public anger, contempt, and outrage while mercilessly mocking liberal thinkers and Democratic politicians in the most venomous terms.

Limbaugh delighted in using the airwaves to expound bigoted, homophobic, and sexist opinions. As *Los Angeles Times* media critic Mary McNamara wrote in Limbaugh's 2021 obituary, "Limbaugh paved the way for a baseline of incivility that has been normalized in political discourse. . . . Limbaugh helped to turn the public discourse in one of the most diverse and successful nations of the world into a competition between two teams: Red vs. Blue, liberals vs. conservatives. Us vs. Them."[27]

Limbaugh's style of firebrand conservative commentary made *The Rush Limbaugh Show* the highest-rated talk radio show in the United States for decades. Limbaugh became a multimillionaire and generated massive profits for iHeartMedia, which distributed the show to over 650 radio stations. By 1994 Limbaugh had 20 million daily listeners, and his show spawned countless imitators that raked in huge profits by selling incivility.

Limbaugh's rise to the top of talk radio would not have been possible in an earlier era. Beginning in 1949 the Federal Com-

Conservative radio talk show host Rush Limbaugh, pictured speaking in 2019, helped normalize incivility in political discourse. His controversial content attracted millions of listeners.

munications Commission (FCC), which regulates radio and television, enforced a rule called the Fairness Doctrine. The policy was based on the idea that the airwaves were a public resource that should serve everyone. Under the Fairness Doctrine, broadcasters were required to present contrasting views on important issues. Those who failed to grant equal time to all sides of an issue could lose their broadcasting license. In 1987 the FCC announced that it would no longer enforce the fairness doctrine; the agency believed the doctrine was no longer necessary, since the rise of cable television had increased the number of channels and therefore viewpoints expressed. Limbaugh was an immediate outgrowth of this change; he used his daily show to promote a singular, one-sided view of American politics.

Politics as Entertainment

Australian media mogul Rupert Murdoch was a beneficiary of Limbaugh's influence on society. Murdoch founded Fox News in

Rooting Rather than Reading

Journalist Matt Taibbi is a harsh critic of cable news networks on both sides of the political divide. In his 2019 book, *Hate Inc.: Why Today's Media Makes Us Despise One Another*, Taibbi says that by 2016, news networks like CNN, Fox News, and MSNBC were covering politics the exact same way they covered sports:

Virtually all the sports graphic ideas had been stolen. There were "countdown to kickoff" clocks for votes, "percent chance of victory" trackers, "our experts pick" charts, a "magic number" for delegate counts, and a hundred different graphic doodads helping us keep score in the game. . . . You could wallpaper the Grand Canyon with debate-coverage boxing clichés. . . . See how often you read/hear one or more of these words in a debate story: "spar," "parry," "jab," "knockout," "knockdown," "glass jaw," "uppercut," "low blow," "counterpunch," "rope-a-dope," "rabbit punch," "sucker punch," "in the ring," "TKO," or any of about a dozen other terms. . . .

[We have] raised a generation of viewers who had no conception of politics as an activity that might or should involve compromise. Your team either won or lost, and you felt devastated or vindicated accordingly. We were training rooters instead of readers.

Matt Taibbi, *Hate Inc.: Why Today's Media Makes Us Despise One Another*. New York: OR Books, 2019, pp. 51–52.

1996 and put Republican operative Roger Ailes in charge. Murdoch and Ailes smashed the idea of watered-down, nonthreatening news programs. Early shows like *Hannity & Colmes* were current events versions of the pro wrestling shows that were growing in popularity at the time. Conservative Sean Hannity played the heel, or bad guy, to wimpy liberal Alan Colmes, who always lost the argument. Social critic Matt Taibbi asserts:

This was theater, not news, and it was not designed to seize the whole audience the way other debate shows like CNN's *Crossfire* were. . . . Rightist anger merchants like Hannity . . . were rapidly [attracting] audiences that were frustrated, white, and often elderly. . . . This was a new model for the media. Instead of targeting the broad [audience], they were now narrowly hunting demographics.[28]

These audiences were extremely popular with advertisers, who spent millions annually on ads targeting Fox viewers.

By the early 2000s one-third of Republicans said they regularly watched Fox News, according to the Pew Research Center. While Fox viewership was soaring, the share of Americans who watched network news shows fell by 15 percent. Meanwhile, the number of people watching CNN fell by 8 percent. Faced with these numbers, news shows began to imitate the Fox News model. Program directors at the cable news network MSNBC decided that if Fox was going to appeal to the right, its shows would appeal to the left. MSNBC's progressive reputation was cemented when *The Rachel Maddow Show* began attracting nearly 2 million viewers nightly after its launch in 2008. Taibbi describes what motivated cable news programmers:

> If you got [a progressive and a conservative] in different rooms watching different channels, you could get both viewers literally addicted to hating one another. . . . We sold anger, and we did it mainly by feeding audiences what they wanted to hear. Mostly, this involved cranking out stories about people our viewers loved to hate. . . . The modern news consumer tuned into news that confirmed his or her prejudices about whatever or whoever the villain of the day happened to be.[29]

Misinforming the Public

Research shows that Fox News and MSNBC audiences are highly partisan. Around 93 percent of Fox viewers are Republicans, while 95 percent of MSNBC viewers say they identify as Democrats, according to a 2021 study by Florida Atlantic University.

While people often think the two partisan cable news networks are equally biased, research shows that Fox News plays a unique role in spreading division and misinformation. A 2021 poll by the Kaiser Family Foundation found that those who get most of their news from Fox are much more likely to believe falsehoods and conspiracy theories promoted by the network's commentators. For example, more than three-quarters of Fox News viewers falsely believe that Democrats stole the 2020 presidential election and that the true winner was Donald Trump. Critics blame Fox News hosts like Hannity, Carlson, and Laura Ingraham for repeating this falsehood hundreds of times on air for months after the election.

Fox viewers are also five times more likely to hear the word *hate* than viewers of MSNBC. The National Research Foundation studied over one thousand transcripts from the two ideologically branded networks during four months in 2020. Hosts on Fox used the word *hate* 647 times, compared to 118 on MSNBC. Fox viewers were told that Democrats, liberals, and elites hate Fox viewers (referred to as "you" and "us"). Liberals were also repeatedly said to hate Christians and Trump voters. The phrase "they hate," in reference to Democrats, was used 101 times compared to just 5 on MSNBC.

Research shows that repeated exposure to such messaging leads viewers to see the opposing party as immoral, unpatriotic, and dangerous. According to a 2019 Pew Research Center poll, 63 percent of Republicans say Democrats are more unpatriotic compared with other Americans. About 23 percent of Democrats say the same about Republicans.

Anger Is Addictive

People on both sides of the political aisle might be forgiven for their tribalism because anger can be addictive. This can be traced back to evolutionary biology. A structure in the brain called the amygdala evolved to release chemical substances when a person experiences danger, fear, and anger. These chemicals, such as

Only Two Sides to Every Story

Corporate media entities follow certain guidelines to keep consumers coming back for more. One strategy is to cover every issue as if there are only two sides: the Republican (red) view or the Democratic (blue) view. But cable news outlets rarely cover the opinions of those who might have a different perspective. For example, the organization FAIR, which analyzes mainstream media, looked at news reporting of the immigration debate for one month in 2021. An analysis of CNN, ABC, Fox News, MSNBC, and other channels showed that 63 percent of those interviewed about the immigration situation on the southern border were current or former government officials expressing mainstream left or right views. Those working in immigration enforcement were also featured.

Video clips of migrants being arrested or walking through the desert provided visuals for the stories. But only 6 percent of people discussing immigration were actual migrants who explained why they left home. And while officials talked at length about immigration problems, migrants who spoke on camera had an average of only one sentence each. News networks showed few Central American scholars or activists who could challenge the standard left/right government views or provide historical context to the immigration issue.

adrenaline, flow into the body whether the danger is a lion attacking or the perceived threat from a member of an opposing political group. Adrenaline heightens awareness, raises blood pressure, and increases the heart rate. A pleasure-inducing chemical called dopamine, released in dangerous situations, makes a person feel strong and invincible. According to Taibbi:

> People become addicted to the dopamine rush of anger that they get from [watching cable news]. And we just sort of sociopathically crank this stuff out there and dump it on audiences without thinking about what it does to their mental health. . . . This product that we're selling—we're selling you your own rage, basically bottled and amplified—it's emotionally destructive in the same way that cigarettes are physiologically destructive.[30]

The more dopamine people get, the more they want. For news viewers, this means spending hours a day glued to their TV sets. But the unhealthy emotional addiction can be worse for those who endlessly scroll through their social media feeds. Social media apps use the same concepts as cable news channels to keep users tuned in and watching ads. When social media users are racking up likes, shares, and followers, they feel gratified as their phones vibrate and light up with new notifications. When notifications do not appear, users craving a dose of dopamine can feel anxious and depressed. Rather than put down the phone, they post again and again, hoping their numbers will increase. This can lead to a social media addiction that can be very hard to break.

When a compulsion to engage with social media is combined with a flood of negative, divisive content, users suffer. But Facebook, Instagram, TikTok, and other sites understand that negative content increases user engagement. This insight was confirmed by former Facebook product manager Frances Haugen in 2021. Haugen released tens of thousands of pages of internal company documents that revealed that Facebook's chief executive officer, Mark Zuckerberg, knows the platform is used to propagate hatred and lies. But company research shows that angry, negative comments attract more likes and shares than posts that are positive. Andrew Selepak, a professor of mass communications at the University of Florida, claims, "[Facebook] feeds us negative content to get us to react negatively. Facebook has realized that to a large extent, we want this experience. We sort of crave this experience and we keep coming back to it for that same type of content. To be riled up."[31]

People who are riled up spend more time scrolling through their Facebook feeds. This leads them to see more advertisements. And Facebook's parent company, Meta, earned over $30 billion in profits in 2021, largely from money

> "[Social media] feeds us negative content to get us to react negatively. . . . We sort of crave this experience and we keep coming back to it . . . to be riled up."[31]
>
> —Andrew Selepak, University of Florida professor of mass communications

paid by advertisers. Some people argue that the profits of Meta, TikTok, Twitter, YouTube, and other social media sites are at the expense of an explosion in incivility.

Amplifying Division

Almost every type of negative, nasty behavior is amplified by social media. Anonymous users feel little restraint when it comes to bullying, making vulgar comments, or even casually tweeting death threats to political opponents. Social media has also helped turn the twenty-first century into the age of conspiracy theories. Outlandish ideas that once circulated among a small group of believers are now accepted as truth by millions of people. A 2021 CNN poll found that around half of all Americans know somebody who believes in a conspiracy theory posted on Facebook. That number is higher among younger Americans; 61 percent of adults younger than thirty-five say they know someone who supports a conspiracy theory based on Facebook content. Perhaps this is not surprising, since social media has taken on the role once played by cable news; 45 percent of Americans say they get their news from Facebook. And research shows that much of that news is not accurate. Divisive articles filled with lies and misinformation generate six times more user engagement than accurate news stories, according to a 2021 study by New York University. Social media companies have little motivation to remove contentious content, since it generates greater profits.

The link between social media and cable news media cannot be overlooked. Intolerance on social media is often fed by stories that originally aired on Fox News and other right-wing outlets like Newsmax and OAN. And while Jon Stewart's criticism of Tucker Carlson did get Carlson fired by CNN, it did not stop the interest in his type of vitriol. Carlson is one of the most divisive figures on cable TV. His political opinion show *Tucker Carlson Tonight* on Fox News promotes conspiracy theories, racist dogma, and misleading claims about COVID-19 vaccines and stolen elections. Despite the ongoing controversies, or perhaps because of them, *Tucker Carlson Tonight* is the highest-rated program in cable news history, attracting a nightly audience of more than 4 million.

In a nation of more than 332 million people, Carlson's audience is little more than 1 percent of the US population. And shows on Fox, CNN, and MSNBC rarely address the beliefs of the 30 to 45 percent of Americans who do not vote in any given year. Some do not care about politics; others think it is all nonsense. But language that is the loudest and sharpest tends to cut through all the noise on cable news and social media. As long as people accept the promoted claim that the left/right rift is the most important social division, the American people will remain divided on almost every newsworthy issue.

CHAPTER FOUR

The Increasingly Ugly World of Politics

Luke O'Neil says his mother is one of the kindest, sweetest people on earth, and he would be nothing without her. But there is one topic O'Neil does not talk about with his mother—politics. O'Neil's mom spends her days watching commentators like Sean Hannity and Tucker Carlson on Fox News. O'Neil says she often repeats racist, homophobic, and antidemocratic statements she hears on her favorite cable news shows. O'Neil, who is a journalist, tweeted about his mother developing what he calls "Fox News brain."[32] His feed was quickly flooded with similar stories from people who no longer spoke to family members or former friends due to the political chasm that had opened between them. They described loved ones as seething with toxic anger while bashing immigrants and repeating outlandish conspiracy theories constantly repeated on cable news.

Ironically, liberals and conservatives do have one thing in common; both sides drop relationships because of political differences. Republican Florida steelworker Ricardo Deforest says he disowned his cousins because they are hard-core Trump haters. "I hate to say it because family is everything. I disowned them. In my mind they're not family anymore,"[33] he asserts.

Liberals and conservatives disagree about many issues, including racial justice, the economy, school curriculum, vaccines, the environment, and the role of law enforcement in society. And these disagreements are creating two separate Americas made up of factions that refuse to speak to one another. A 2020 poll from the Pew Research Center demonstrates this point: 80 percent of Americans have just a few or no friends on the other side of the political aisle.

The Art of Compromise

People living through today's political polarization might believe it has always been this way. But this is not the case. It was once commonly said that politics is the art of compromise; while politicians fought over issues, they were willing to make some concessions to the other side. For decades Republicans and Democrats generally worked together in a bipartisan fashion to do what was best for the country. When Democrat Barack Obama was elected president in 2008, he praised the idea of working across party lines and even nominated two Republicans to his cabinet. Obama was able to sign a few important pieces of bipartisan legislation, including a tax deal and employment legislation known as the JOBS Act. As Obama said after his term ended in 2017, "Bipartisanship is a virtue if we, both sides, [say,] 'Look, we have a problem. We may differ on how we solve it, but let's sit down and negotiate.' And there's never been an issue in Washington that I haven't been willing to take a half-loaf or a quarter-loaf."[34]

Not all Democrats were happy with Obama's spirit of compromise. This was especially true after Republican Senate majority leader Mitch McConnell said in 2010, "The single most important thing [Republicans] want to achieve is for President Obama to be a one-term president."[35] Those who followed McConnell's

The news has become increasingly polarized in recent years, and political disagreements between friends and family members can become so heated that people even stop talking to one another.

plan refused to compromise with Democrats on any legislation because they did not want the American public to see the president succeeding. But McConnell failed to prevent Obama from winning a second term in 2012.

The Insult President

One of the most shocking acts of political incivility during Obama's presidency occurred in 2009 during the State of the Union address. As Obama addressed the assembled lawmakers and cabinet members about his proposed health care plan, South Carolina Republican representative Joe Wilson yelled out, "You lie!"[36] While it might be hard to believe in 2022 that this was considered a major breach of etiquette, the House passed a resolution admonishing Wilson for the remark. But in a preview of what was to become standard procedure for uncivil politicians, Wilson used the notoriety to quickly raise $2.5 million for his reelection campaign.

Cold Feelings Prevail

Americans have always divided along political lines. But the small divisions seen in the past have now turned into a deep political chasm, according to researchers at the American National Election Studies. In 1978 the organization set up a polling method to rate how Americans felt about each political party on a scale from 0 (very cold) to 100 (very warm). Up until the late 1990s, each party received a score right around 50, which showed that Republicans and Democrats basically accepted one another. Even in 2000 only around 10 percent gave the opposing party a 0. But since that time, the divide has been growing. In 2020 around half of Republicans rated the Democratic Party at 0 on the 0–100 scale. This is a 600 percent increase in twenty years. Slightly fewer Democrats, 38 percent, gave Republicans a 0 rating, which is an increase of around 400 percent.

Beyond the numbers, members of each party see the opposition as dangerous; 64 percent of Democrats believe Republicans pose a serious threat to the country. Among Republicans, 75 percent believe Democratic beliefs threaten the very existence of the country.

Few politicians have reaped greater rewards for incivility than Republican Donald Trump. Before he ran for president in 2016, Trump never held public office. But he understood competition better than most, thanks to his years as a high-stakes New York real estate developer and as the host and executive producer of the popular reality show *The Apprentice* from 2004 to 2015. Trump saw that successful contestants on *The Apprentice* generated widespread interest on social media. The most popular participants were unpredictable, egotistical, and supremely confident in their beliefs. They insulted and offended people and never apologized. Winning was the only goal, and successful contestants said and did whatever was necessary to mercilessly destroy their opponents. Media studies professor June Deery claims that Trump's strategy for winning the presidential election was based on approaching the political process as a reality show. "Trump's learned that to get attention—which is everything in politics—it's best to be the most outrageous person in the room," she argues. "[In reality TV] extroverted pushy personalities come to the fore."[37]

When it came to being outrageous in his pursuit of political power, Trump spared no one. Trump used Twitter as a weapon to insult Democrats, Republicans, his own cabinet members, journalists, celebrities, and late-night talk show hosts. Trump's insult Tweets between 2015 to 2021 numbered in the thousands, according to a list compiled by the *New York Times*. When referring to Republicans who crossed him, Trump constantly used the terms *weak*, *stupid*, *pathetic*, *crazy*, *failing*, and *losers*. On numerous occasions, Trump called Democrats corrupt, crooked, total failures, crime-loving, very sick, freaks, and sleazy. Trump often targeted certain women as well, using terms like *crazy*, *low-IQ*, *fat pigs*, and *horseface*. He described the mainstream media as fake news and repeatedly called journalists enemies of the people.

Charges of Racism

No president had ever spurned the rules of civility like Trump, and critics accused him of normalizing the language of racism. Victims of Trump's Twitter tirades included Black athletes, congresswomen of color, Muslims, Mexican immigrants, and Africans. In 2020, during the George Floyd antiracist demonstrations, some storefronts in New York City were damaged and contents stolen as BLM protesters took to the streets. Trump tweeted that "New York was lost to the looters, thugs, Radical Left, and all other forms of Lowlife & Scum." Reporters pointed out that those terms have long been used by racists against Black people who were demanding equal rights. Trump answered, as he often had in the past, that he is "the least racist person there is anywhere in the world."[38]

Trump's uncivil language often had real-world consequences. After the president began calling the COVID-19 virus the "kung flu" and the "China virus" on Twitter, anti-Asian hate crimes soared across the country. According to media reports compiled by the

New York Times, people of Asian descent were threatened, physically assaulted, spit on, targeted with racial slurs, and told to "go back to China" and that "you are the virus."[39] Some of the victims of physical assault included a ninety-one-year-old man in Oakland, California, and an eighty-nine-year-old woman in Brooklyn, New York. The episodes were not limited to the coasts. In 2020 there were thirty-eight hundred anti-Asian racist incidents across nearly every state in the country.

Several government reports and academic studies in 2021 linked Trump's insults and intolerance to the rise in racial hatred. FBI data shows that anti-Asian hate crimes surged 145 percent in the largest US cities in 2020 after dropping continuously for the previous twenty-five years. A report by the *American Journal of Public Health* blamed Trump for a surge in anti-Asian hashtags appearing on social media. According to the study, Trump's tweet about the "Chinese virus" on March 16, 2020, "was directly re-

After Trump called COVID-19 the "kung flu" and the "China virus," anti-Asian hate crimes surged. This picture shows a memorial outside the Aromatherapy Spa in Atlanta, Georgia, where a woman was shot and killed.

sponsible for a major increase in anti-Asian hashtags . . . and the use of terms like 'Chinese virus' and 'kung flu,' which Trump publicly said at a rally in June (2020), have come alongside a rise in racist sentiment toward Asians in the U.S."[40]

Polls show that Trump's vicious language has had an enduring negative effect on civil society. In a 2021 poll taken by the Public Religion Research Institute, one-third of Republican voters said that "true American patriots might have to resort to violence to save our country." Only one in ten Democrats agreed with this statement. Robert Jones, founder of the institute, expressed alarm at this finding: "I've been doing this a while, for decades, and it's not the kind of finding that as a sociologist, a public opinion pollster, that you're used to seeing."[41]

Rewarding Intolerance

While Trump was widely criticized for his rude, crude, unpresidential language, many of his supporters loved it because it was unvarnished and not laced with the platitudes and double-talk that politicians are commonly accused of spouting. Others simply liked the brazenness of the messages. Trump held hundreds of rallies before, during, and after his presidency, which ended in early 2021, and crowds cheered at nearly every uncivilized remark. And the former president's belligerent style of politics is being mimicked by politicians across the country. In 2022 a Republican congressional candidate in Virginia—supported by Trump—said that anyone convicted of voter fraud should be arrested and executed. While his tweet got him banned from Twitter, the candidate was publicly endorsed by Trump and was supported by most members of his party.

One of the fastest-rising stars in Republican politics also called for executions in 2022. Arizona state senator Wendy Rogers gained national attention when she advocated hanging state officials who certified Joseph Biden's win in the 2020 presidential election. "We need to build more gallows," she announced. "If we try some of these high-level criminals, convict them and use a newly built set of gallows, it'll make an example

Follow

Donald J. Trump

@realDonaldTrump

45th President of the United States of America🇺🇸

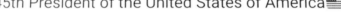 Washington, DC 🔗 Vote.DonaldJTrump.com
 Joined March 2009

51 Following   88.7M Followers

Tweets   Tweets & replies   Media   Likes

of these traitors who have betrayed our country."[42] At the time, Rogers was speaking to an audience of openly racist White nationalists.

Rogers's career trajectory demonstrates the rewards of amplifying intolerance and conflict. She began her political career as a traditional conservative in 2010 but failed to get elected on five occasions. When Rogers was running for the Arizona state senate in 2020, she came out as a loyal Trump supporter who backed extremist ideologies. In a move that helped her rise from political obscurity, Rogers began promoting White nationalist ideas on her six social media accounts. This move quickly attracted more than seven hundred thousand followers. This helped Rogers raise more than $1 million for her political campaign, mostly through small donations that flowed in from outside the state. After winning in 2020 and again in 2022, she was able to raise $2.5 million on social media. This amount surpassed every other candidate for Arizona state office and helped Rogers gain national recognition. Phoenix Republican election attorney Chris Rose opposes Rogers's brand of politics but admits it is effective: "It used to be that if someone said something crazy, they would get slapped down by the party leaders in a way that could hurt. Now it's a badge of honor if people are mad at you."[43]

After several weeks of political pressure from Democratic politicians, the Republican majority in the Arizona senate voted to censure Rogers for promoting violence. (A censure expresses disapproval for someone, but that person is not fined or punished in any way.) Rogers vowed to personally destroy any Republicans who moved against her, but Republican Arizona senate president Karen Fann supported the censure. "We do support First Amendment freedom of speech," Fann says. "But what we do not condone is members threatening each other, to ruin each other, to incite violence, to call us communists. We don't do that to each other. We, as elected officials, are held to a higher standard."[44]

Targeting Politicians

While Fann might believe elected officials should be held to a higher standard, some of Rogers's supporters did not agree. Politicians who voted for censure received numerous vile comments and death threats from Rogers's online followers. And the normalization of violent political rhetoric has created an atmosphere of anxiety among politicians, administrators, and election officials of both major parties.

Trolls dox politicians they do not like, posting their addresses, phone numbers, and other personal information online. Anonymous callers and texters use this information to target politicians with obscenities and racist slurs. Some threaten to hunt down and kill officials, their spouses, and their children.

Women are ten times more likely to be harassed this way, according to a study by the Institute for Strategic Dialogue.

Some of those targeted have police guarding their homes, while others have been forced to hire private security guards. Victims of harassment have moved into temporary housing to avoid armed protesters outside their homes. They have canceled family gatherings after death threats and picked up guns for self-protection.

In this heated political environment, the number of threats against members of Congress jumped more than fourfold, according to US Capitol Police records. In 2016 the US Capitol Police investigated 902 threats. The following year, after Trump's election, that number reached 3,939. In 2021 threats against politicians reached a record high of more than 9,600.

Who Is to Blame?

Some believe this uncivil war can be blamed on the American public. For example, journalist Isadora Rangel writes, "Civility can only be achieved when we look at our behavior first. If the majority of us weren't engaged on some level in uncivil behavior, then we wouldn't have the issue in the first place."[45] But politicians understand that stoking an uncivil war can be beneficial for their careers. And they only have to look to Trump as an example. He sent out angry, divisive tweets almost every day of his presidency. When critics howled, he used their criticism against him as a badge of honor in fund-raising letters that helped him raise hundreds of millions of dollars. This strategy also boosted turnout in elections; the two presidential elections with Trump on the ballot had some of the highest voter participation in more than a century. As journalist David Lauter writes, "In theory, a candidate can achieve extremely large turnouts based on positive emotions, like pride or hope—then-candidate Barack Obama achieved record turnout [in 2008] among Black voters on

"Anger and division provide the fastest route to high [voter] turnout; unity almost always dampens political engagement."[46]

—David Lauter, *Los Angeles Times* senior editor

Embattled Women in Politics

In 2021 there was a record number of Black women in government. While this achievement was widely celebrated, these representatives were also harassed and threatened in record numbers. While there are no exact figures, PBS reporter Candice Norwood spoke with eighteen Black women at all levels of government, and seventeen said they had been targets of verbal abuse and physical threats. As Connecticut representative Jahana Hayes reports, "I remember, at the beginning of the 116th Congress [January 2019], when we were just spotlighting and highlighting the beautiful diversity of this incoming Congress, but then . . . we had members who were getting death threats on a daily basis."

The threats are often too much for some to bear. Former Vermont legislator Kiah Morris says she suffered years of harassment before resigning in 2018. "This is an incredibly crushing weight to carry on a daily basis," she says. "It is mentally exhausting to live in constant fear, feeling like you're in a state of constant fight or flight, and not knowing who to trust." While harassment is common, some are reluctant to speak out. They say that when they talk about the abuse, they often see an increase in the number of threats they receive on social media.

Quoted in Amna Nawaz et al., "For Black Women in Government, Highlighting Threats and Abuse Can Make It Worse," *PBS NewsHour*, June 29, 2021. www.pbs.org.

that basis, for example. But anger and division provide the fastest route to high turnout; unity almost always dampens political engagement."[46]

While high turnout might boost a politician's fortunes, there is ample evidence from history that violent political rhetoric can lead to actual violence. When politicians use despicable, dehumanizing words against their opponents, they are blazing a dangerous path to a violent future that they will not be able to control.

CHAPTER FIVE

Stepping Back from Anger

In November 2021 students at the University of Pennsylvania were offered a class called Civil Dialogue Seminar: Civic Engagement in a Divided Nation. Because of pandemic restrictions, discussion sessions were held on Zoom. During a conversation about US immigration policy, two of the fifty participants got into a heated discussion. An unnamed White male student took a common conservative position that undocumented immigrants were using taxpayer resources that should be reserved for Americans. A Latina student named Alejandra pushed back. She described the hardships her parents had faced as undocumented immigrants from El Salvador. Because they were not in the country legally, they could not access government resources like affordable medical insurance, food stamps, or other federal programs available to citizens. The male student stuck to his position, replying that every country has a right to secure its borders. Alejandra became so emotional she turned off her camera, took some deep breaths, and tried to calm down.

When Alejandra returned to the conversation, something unexpected happened. The male student said he was sorry if he had offended her. Alejandra replied, "I really appreciate you saying that. I wanted to dismiss what you were saying, but your perspective helped me think about the ways that I can bring more awareness to these issues."[47]

The Civil Dialogue Seminar is one of a growing number of similar courses, orientation programs, and workshops offered by colleges since the late 2010s. These initiatives are meant to encourage free speech and find common ground on divisive issues. College students are increasingly supportive of these attempts to heal the nation's political polarization. According to a 2022 Knight Foundation–Ipsos study on free expression and campus speech, 84 percent of all college students say free speech rights are critically important to a healthy democracy. However, a declining share believe free speech rights are secure. In 2015 more than 70 percent of students said freedom of speech was very secure in the United States. In 2021 only 47 percent believed this to be true. Much of the decline came from Republican students who felt less secure about expressing their opinions around liberals on campus. There was also a racial divide concerning free speech issues; 90 percent of White students felt that they were protected by the First Amendment right to free speech. Only 60 percent of Black students said they felt safe freely voicing their opinions.

In 2021 academic researchers at the Bipartisan Policy Center released a document to address free speech issues in school settings. *Campus Free Expression: A New Roadmap* seeks to promote civil dialogue and expose students to diverse opinions. Pilot programs in the document focus on creating a more inclusive culture among faculty, athletes, members of fraternities and sororities, and the student body in general. The executive summary of *Campus Free Expression: A New Roadmap* explains its purpose: "We cannot afford for higher education to become another scene of deep partisan division. As a country, we must be better at robustly and respectfully debating difficult issues across the political spectrum, and college campuses have an essential role in achieving this civic goal."[48]

Students Advocate for Civility

Some students are not waiting to get to college to push back on divisive partisan scenes in their communities. While adults sometimes turn school board meetings into shouting matches, students are standing together to promote civil discourse on difficult subjects. This was the case in York, Pennsylvania, in 2021. The roots of the controversy were planted after the 2020 George Floyd BLM protests. To address issues such as systemic racism, York teachers created a list of books, articles, and movies that teachers could use as a resource to teach high school students Black history and antiracism. However, within a few months the school board voted to ban the resources from being used in classrooms. This was based on protests by two school board members who falsely believed the materials were meant to teach White students that they should feel bad about themselves because they would be depicted as racists. The meeting was attended by adults. Some supported the ban, while others spoke out against it.

In September 2021 a group of York high school seniors formed a group called the Panther Anti-Racist Union (PARU) to exercise their civil right to protest. Every day, around twenty-five protesters

A student participates in an online class. Colleges are offering a growing number of courses and workshops meant to encourage free speech and help students find common ground on divisive issues.

Promoting Free Expression on Campus

In 2021 a document called *Campus Free Expression: A New Roadmap* was released by the Bipartisan Policy Center. The executive summary, excerpted below, explains the importance of free speech in civil society:

> The chilling of campus speech is having effects beyond the borders of the campus. Rather than alleviating the political polarization in our nation today, the inhibition of campus speech is degrading the civic mission of higher education, which is to maintain our pluralistic democracy by preparing students for civic participation as independent thinkers who can tolerate contrary viewpoints and work constructively with those with whom they have principled disagreements. . . .
>
> Colleges and universities should elevate the skills and dispositions necessary to academic and civic discourse as a deliberate aim of the collegiate experience. Formal protections for free expression are necessary but insufficient to create a culture of free expression, open inquiry, and respectful, productive debate on campus and in our country. We have a national civic skills deficit, which colleges and universities have an essential role in remedying. . . . Our aim should be to graduate students who raise the bar for national discourse.

Jim Douglas et al., *Campus Free Expression: A New Roadmap*, Bipartisan Policy Center, 2021. https://bipartisanpolicy.org.

held signs and chanted slogans in front of their school at 7:15 a.m. as parents dropped off students and school buses arrived. PARU founder Edha Gupta explained why she was protesting. "It's our classrooms, what we're being taught . . . so if anything, I think we should have the biggest hand in what we're learning," she maintained. "It hurts me to see my peers learning inaccurate things, or not enough things or a half-right and half-wrong view of history."[49]

After several months of protests, the students were successful. In early 2022 the York school board reinstated the resource list. Sixteen-year-old PARU member Renee Ellis said of the type of education she wants to experience in the classroom, "[I] think learning basic human decency—as naive as that sounds—is lacking. Why can't we learn how to discuss and have good political conversations with one another and be civil about things? We want to learn about what civics is, what our civic duty is, but we don't learn how to be civil."[50]

Moms Moved to Act

Students are not the only ones hoping to highlight civility in educational matters. In Ohio a group of suburban moms are organizing national training sessions for those who wish to counter the anger breaking out at school board meetings. Katie Paris founded the Red Wine & Blue network in 2018 to teach de-escalation tactics to like-minded suburban moms. The group highlights the type of civil political conversations women might have with each other while sharing a bottle of wine. Paris, who is a mother of two, believes this could counter groups of irate individuals who are disrupting school board meetings and in some cases threatening officials over mask mandates and curriculum controversies.

Red Wine & Blue started out as an Ohio-based organization, but by 2022 the group had grown to include more than three hun-

Katie Paris speaks to members of Red Wine & Blue during a 2020 meeting in Cleveland. She founded the Red Wine & Blue network in 2018 to teach de-escalation tactics to like-minded suburban mothers.

dred thousand women from across the country. Red Wine & Blue holds training sessions on Zoom, where members are instructed on the best ways to make their points in a civil manner. They are told to prepare fact-based speeches before attending school board meetings. Divisive words like *critical race theory* are to be avoided; instead, lessons should be referred to as "culturally responsive instruction."[51] Other civil tactics include presenting a calm face in tense situations and waving hands like a jazz dancer instead of applauding or cheering at meetings.

Red Wine & Blue was particularly troubled by the number of books being banned for content some see as objectionable. According to the American Library Association (ALA), more than 330 books were challenged across the United States in the last three months of 2021. This compares with 377 cases for all of 2019. Most of these books included portrayals of racism, LGBTQ lives, the Holocaust, and other issues. The ALA calls the number of book bans unprecedented.

To counter the school board book battles, Red Wine & Blue launched the Book Ban Busters. The website tracks bans in every city and state and provides information to help members testify against the prohibitions at meetings filled with angry attendees. Paris believes that organized, cheerful moms are making a difference. "What we've seen consistently . . . really work [all across the country] is having that decorum! It creates such a contrast with the other side,"[52] she says.

Workshops for Lawmakers

While moms, students, and other citizens work to turn down the temperature at public meetings, the National Institute for Civil Discourse (NICD) offers training programs to those who might need it the most—politicians. The NICD Next Generation program holds weekend-long workshops to help state-level politicians learn to increase civility in their legislatures. By 2022 legislators in seventeen states had attended workshops in which lawmakers told their personal stories and explained how their political views were shaped by their experiences. Group exercises focus on building trust through private conversations with political opponents.

It might sound like common sense to prompt politicians from both sides of the aisle to get to know one another. People who are friendly with one another can often overcome political differences. But in today's hostile political climate, many politicians do not reach out to the opposition to solve problems.

In 2019 Sara Gideon, Democratic House Speaker in Maine, attended an NICD workshop and put some of the recommendations into action. One move was extremely controversial; changing the House seating plan so Democrats and Republicans sat next to one another instead of staying in their own segregated groups. Almost everyone was upset. Democrats did not want to

Sara Gideon is pictured speaking to reporters in 2020. As Democratic House Speaker in Maine, she attempted to increase civility by changing the House seating plan so that Democrats and Republicans were forced to sit next to one another.

Podcasts for That

With an increasing number of students and youth leaders working to promote civil discourse, podcasters are joining the movement. In 2022 Arizona State University's School of Civil and Economic Thought and Leadership (SCETL) launched the *Keeping It Civil* podcast to create a space for civil debate on divisive issues. The program is hosted by law professor Joshua Sellers and political science professor Henry Thomson. The professors interview authors, researchers, scholars, and others who hold varying opinions on topics such as voting rights, systemic racism, and free speech on campus. The podcast is part of SCETL's Civil Discourse Project, which brings speakers to campuses who represent a wide range of political perspectives. The director of SCETL, Paul Carrese, believes the *Keeping It Civil* podcast is necessary because of the unique setting. "It is a university—it's not a public park, it's not a political campaign," he says. "It's a distinctive kind of [academic setting] meant to be more reasonable, meant to be more civil than other spaces of disagreement."

Quoted in Marcia Paterman Brookey, "'Keeping It Civil' Podcast Dedicated to Improving Civil Discourse," ASU News, March 16, 2022. https://news.asu.edu.

sit next to Republicans and vice versa. This only demonstrated to Gideon how much her new seating plan was needed. She says everyone soon got over it, adding, "There's no better sight than when I look out from the speaker's rostrum and see a group of Republicans and Democrats who sit in a couple of rows together, laughing together. It . . . sounds a little silly—but it's just an amazing, great sight."[53]

Gideon, who began her second term as the House Speaker in Maine in 2022, says that presiding over emotional, contentious debates is one of the hardest parts of her job. But she believes the NICD lessons she has put into action have helped lawmakers see each other as more human; they do not automatically think the worst of their political opponents.

> "There's no better sight than when I look out from the speaker's rostrum and see a group of Republicans and Democrats who sit in a couple of rows together, laughing together. . . . It's just an amazing, great sight."[53]
>
> —Sara Gideon, Maine House Speaker

One of Gideon's colleagues, Republican state senator Matt Pouliot, has taken on a role in the NICD, hosting workshops. Pouliot says politicians who use insults to make headlines are at fault, but everyone is responsible for the lower level of civility. "When we don't pay attention unless somebody really makes some type of an obscene outcry, we're all to blame," he states. "And I think that oftentimes we want to blame political figures . . . for the problems that we're seeing in government—but our government is a function of what it is that we want."[54]

Raising Civility Levels

The NICD calls its workshops Next Generation for a reason: state legislators are often referred to as "the farm team" because they are minor league players in training. Some might run for Congress and take their civility experiences to Washington, DC. And the institute was one of over two hundred organizations in 2022 that were working to raise civility at every level of society. Student-based groups like the Bridge Alliance, Civics Unplugged, iCivics, Youth Leadership Initiative, and Up to Us utilize social media, podcasts, and online and in-person workshops to teach young adults how to discuss important issues in a sensitive and civil manner.

Civility workshops are needed now more than ever, according to numerous polls. Anywhere from 70 to 80 percent of Americans from both parties tell pollsters that the level of civility has seriously deteriorated since 2015. While civility workshops might not be able to compete with the bad-mannered masses on social media, earnest problem solvers have a basic truth working for them: most people who get to know each other act civilly to one another. And unless there is a space for people to respectfully disagree, problems large and small will remain unsolved.

Introduction: The Anger Pandemic

1. Quoted in Elizabeth Chang, "Americans Are Living in a Big 'Anger Incubator.' Experts Have Tips for Regulating Our Rage," *Washington Post*, June 30, 2020. www.washingtonpost.com.
2. Quoted in Sarah Lyall, "A Nation on Hold Wants to Speak with a Manger," *New York Times*, January 1, 2022. www.nytimes.com.
3. Quoted in Lyall, "A Nation on Hold Wants to Speak with a Manger."
4. Quoted in Chang, "Americans Are Living in a Big 'Anger Incubator.'"
5. Quoted in Chang, "Americans Are Living in a Big 'Anger Incubator.'"

Chapter One: What Is Civility, and Why Does It Matter?

6. ZZ Packer, "When Is 'Civility' a Duty, and When Is It a Trap?," *New York Times Magazine*, November 28, 2018. www.nytimes.com.
7. Quoted in Packer, "When Is 'Civility' a Duty, and When Is It a Trap?"
8. Packer, "When Is 'Civility' a Duty, and When Is It a Trap?"
9. Martin Luther King Jr., "Letter from a Birmingham Jail," California State University, Chico, 2022. www.csuchico.edu.
10. King, "Letter from a Birmingham Jail."
11. Quoted in Carrie Levine, "New Anti-Protest Laws Cast a Long Shadow on First Amendment Rights," Center for Public Integrity, December 20, 2021. https://publicintegrity.org.
12. Alex Zamalin, *Against Civility*. New York: Beacon, 2021, p. 9.
13. Packer, "When Is 'Civility' a Duty, and When Is It a Trap?"
14. American Civil Liberties Union of Tennessee, *Stand Up/Speak Up: A Guide for Youth Activists*, 2015. www.aclu-tn.org.
15. Quoted in Leila Fadel, "In These Divided Times, Is Civility Under Siege?," NPR, March 12, 2019. www.npr.org.

Chapter Two: Americans Behaving Badly

16. Quoted in Claire Lampen, "Brawl Breaks Out over Golden Corral's Signature Sirloin," *The Cut* (blog), February 2, 2022. www.thecut.com.
17. Quoted in Kerry Breen, "'A Vicious Cycle': Food Workers Speak Out About Confrontations During the Pandemic," *Today*, July 7, 2021. www.today.com.
18. Quoted in Breen, "'A Vicious Cycle.'"
19. Quoted in Alex Abad-Santos, "The Appeal and Futility of Mask Meltdown Videos," Vox, July 9, 2020. www.vox.com.
20. Quoted in Caroline Smith, "'We Know Who You Are.' Group Threatens Doctors, Others Wearing Masks Outside Williamson Co. School Board Meeting," NewsChannel5, August 11, 2021. www.newschannel5.com.

21. Quoted in Stephen Sawchuk, "Why School Boards Are Now Hot Spots for Nasty Politics," *Education Week*, July 29, 2021. www.edweek.org.
22. Quoted in Gabriella Borter et al., "School Boards Get Death Threats Amid Rage over Race, Gender, Mask Policies," Reuters, February 15, 2022. www.reuters.com.
23. Adam Laats, "School Board Meetings Used to Be Boring. Why Have They Become War Zones?," *Washington Post*, September 29, 2021. www.washingtonpost.com.
24. Quoted in Sarah Smith, "We're Losing Our Humanity and the Pandemic Is to Blame," ProPublica, October 7, 2021. www.propublica.org.

Chapter Three: Cable News and Social Media Instigators

25. Quoted in Jennifer Wood, "Jon Stewart Verbally Annihilated Tucker Carlson on His Own Show in 2004—and Many People Are Just Seeing It Now," Uproxx, May 5, 2021. https://uproxx.com.
26. Quoted in Zack Beauchamp, "Watch One of Jon Stewart's Most Famous Moments: His Epic *Crossfire* Appearance," Vox, February 10, 2015. www.vox.com.
27. Mary McNamara, "Column: Rush Limbaugh Died as He Lived—Dividing America," *Los Angeles Times*, February 17, 2021. www.latimes.com.
28. Matt Taibbi, *Hate Inc.: Why Today's Media Makes Us Despise One Another*. New York: OR Books, 2019, p. 19.
29. Taibbi, *Hate Inc.*, p. 21.
30. Quoted in Doug Gordon, "Journalist Matt Taibbi Explains How Following the News Can Be Hazardous to Your Health," Wisconsin Public Radio, March 16, 2019. www.wpr.org.
31. Quoted in Jamey Tucker, "What the Tech? How Facebook Makes You Angry," WRCB, October 6, 2021. www.wrcbtv.com.

Chapter Four: The Increasingly Ugly World of Politics

32. Luke O'Neil, "I Hate What They've Done to Almost Everyone in My Family," Welcome to Hell World, April 5, 2019. https://luke.substack.com.
33. Quoted in Tovia Smith, "'Dude, I'm Done': When Politics Tears Families and Friendships Apart," NPR, October 27, 2020. www.npr.org.
34. Quoted in Christi Parsons and Lisa Mascaro, "Obama, Who Sought to Ease Partisanship, Saw It Worsen Instead," *Los Angeles Times*, January 14, 2017. www.latimes.com.
35. Quoted in Glenn Kessler, "When Did McConnell Say He Wanted to Make Obama a 'One-Term President'?," *Washington Post*, September 25, 2012. www.washingtonpost.com.
36. Quoted in Halimah Abdullah, "Obama Interrupted: Disrespectful or Latest in 'Era of Incivility'?," CNN, June 15, 2012. www.cnn.com.
37. Quoted in Olivia Goldhill, "Five Reality TV Show Strategies Donald Trump Has Used Throughout His Campaign," Quartz, November 6, 2016. https://qz.com.

38. Quoted in Andrea González-Ramírez, "The Ever-Growing List of Trump's Most Racist Rants," *Medium*, 2020. https://gen.medium.com.
39. Quoted in Weiyi Cai et al., "Swelling Anti-Asian Violence: Who Is Being Attacked Where," *New York Times*, April 3, 2021. www.nytimes.com.
40. Quoted in Jin Kai, "How Trump Fueled Anti-Asian Violence in America," The Diplomat, June 8, 2021. https://thediplomat.com.
41. Quoted in Adam Gabbatt, "Almost One in Three Republicans Say Violence May Be Necessary to 'Save' US," *The Guardian* (Manchester, UK), November 1, 2021. www.theguardian.com.
42. Quoted in Jim Small, "Wendy Rogers Said White Nationalists Are 'Patriots' and Called for Hanging Political Enemies," AZ Mirror, February 26, 2022. www.azmirror.com.
43. Quoted in Beth Reinhard and Rosalind S. Helderman, "Arizona Lawmaker Speaks to White Nationalists, Calls for Violence—and Sets Fundraising Records," *Washington Post*, March 8, 2022. www.washingtonpost.com.
44. Quoted in Jeremy Duda, "Senate Votes to Censure Wendy Rogers for Threatening Her Colleagues," AZ Mirror, March 1, 2022. www.azmirror.com.
45. Quoted in Alex Zamalin, "The Case Against Civility in Politics," Literary Hub, February 7, 2022. https://lithub.com.
46. David Lauter, "US Uniting on Ukraine Is a Problem for Trump," *Los Angeles Times*, March 19, 2022. https://enewspaper.latimes.com.

Chapter Five: Stepping Back from Anger

47. Quoted in Jennifer Miller, "Good Talk," *Washington Post Magazine*, March 16, 2022. www.washingtonpost.com.
48. Jim Douglas et al., *Campus Free Expression: A New Roadmap*, Bipartisan Policy Center, 2021. https://bipartisanpolicy.org.
49. Quoted in Gabriela Martinez, "PA Students Protest School Board's Ban on Anti-Racist Teaching Materials," WITF, September 10, 2021. www.witf.org.
50. Quoted in Anne Branigin, "These Students Helped Overturn a Book Ban. Now They're Pushing for a More Inclusive Education," *Washington Post*, February 24, 2022. www.washingtonpost.com.
51. Quoted in Annie Gowen, "'Blue' Suburban Moms Are Mobilizing to Counter Conservatives in Fights over Masks, Book Bans and Diversity Education," *Washington Post*, February 9, 2022. www.washingtonpost.com.
52. Quoted in Gowen, "'Blue' Suburban Moms Are Mobilizing to Counter Conservatives in Fights over Masks, Book Bans and Diversity Education."
53. Quoted in Sarah McCammon, "Can We Come Together? How Americans Are Trying to Talk Across the Divide," NPR, April 4, 2019. www.npr.org.
54. Quoted in McCammon, "Can We Come Together?"

Books

Stuart A. Kallen, *Protest: A History of Social Movements in America*. San Diego: ReferencePoint, 2022.

Jamie Margolin, *Youth to Power: Your Voice and How to Use It*. New York: Hachette, 2020.

Jason Reynolds and Ibram X. Kendi, *Racism, Antiracism, and You*. Boston: Little, Brown, 2020.

Matt Taibbi, *Hate Inc.: Why Today's Media Makes Us Despise One Another*. New York: OR Books, 2019.

Alex Zamalin, *Against Civility*. Boston: Beacon, 2021.

Internet Sources

Alex Abad-Santos, "The Appeal and Futility of Mask Meltdown Videos," Vox, July 9, 2020. www.vox.com.

Kerry Breen, "'A Vicious Cycle': Food Workers Speak Out About Confrontations During the Pandemic," *Today*, July 7, 2021. www.today.com.

Elizabeth Chang, "Americans Are Living in a Big 'Anger Incubator.' Experts Have Tips for Regulating Our Rage," *Washington Post*, June 30, 2020. www.washingtonpost.com.

Sarah Lyall, "A Nation on Hold Wants to Speak with a Manger," *New York Times*, January 1, 2022. www.nytimes.com.

Jennifer Miller, "Good Talk," *Washington Post Magazine*, March 16, 2022. www.washingtonpost.com.

ZZ Packer, "When Is 'Civility' a Duty, and When Is It a Trap?," *New York Times Magazine*, November 28, 2018. www.nytimes.com.

Shankar Vedantam, "How Rude!" Hidden Brain (podcast), April 11, 2022. https://hidden-brain.simplecast.com/episodes/how-rude-jnzZ VvUy.

Websites

Bipartisan Policy Center

https://bipartisanpolicy.org

This Washington, DC, think tank works to foster cooperation between the two major political parties. The Campus Free Expression section is focused on offering solutions to students who wish to participate in a healthy democracy.

Bridge Alliance

www.bridgealliance.us

The Bridge Alliance is a coalition of one hundred groups dedicated to improving civil discourse while encouraging all Americans to participate in the political process. More than a dozen of the groups are for students and young adults.

Civic Online Reasoning

https://cor.stanford.edu

This learning framework hosted by Stanford University offers curriculum, videos, and other tools to better inform students about civic matters by teaching methods fact-checkers use to evaluate the trustworthiness of online sources.

iCivics

www.icivics.org

iCivics is dedicated to supporting quality student civics education at every grade level. The website includes learning materials, more than a dozen games, and a library focused on government, the US Constitution, and the workings of the legislative branch.

National Constitution Center

https://constitutioncenter.org

The National Constitution Center brings together liberals and conservatives to civilly debate constitutional issues on all media platforms. The website offers educational materials, videos, and other resources aimed at helping students engage in civic matters.

National Institute for Civil Discourse

https://nicd.arizona.edu

This organization at the University of Arizona offers several programs to increase bipartisanship, collaboration, and civility in schools, government, and society. The group's website offers videos, studies, and articles with a focus on civility.

Note: Boldface page numbers indicate illustrations.

Abrams, David, 20
adrenaline, 32–33
Against Civility (Zamalin), 14
Ailes, Roger, 30
air rage, 21
American Journal of Public Health, 42
American Library Association (ALA), 53
American National Election Studies, 40
amygdala, 32
anger
    addictive nature of, 32–35
    cable news promotes, 31
    election turnout and, 46–47
    expression at school board meetings, 24–25
    negative health effects of, 5–6
    over mask mandates, 19–21
anti-Asian rhetoric/hate crimes, 42–43
anti-protest laws, 13–15
Apprentice, The (TV program), 40
Aristotle, 9
Arizona State University, 55
Armed Conflict Location & Event Data Project (ACLED), 13
Aromatherapy Spa shooting (Atlanta), **42**

Begala, Paul, 26
Biden, Joe, 43
Bipartisan Policy Center, 49, 61
Black Lives Matter (BLM) movement, 13, 41
    percentage of youth participating in, 25
Book Ban Busters, 53

book bans, 53
Bridge Alliance, 56, 61
Bureau of Labor Statistics, 19
Bybee, Keith, 16

Campus Free Expression (Bipartisan Policy Center), 49
Cardona, Annabelle, 5
Carlson, Tucker, 26, 32, 36
charity, Americans' donations to, 7
Civic Online Reasoning, 61
Civics Unplugged, 56
Civil Dialogue Seminar (University of Pennsylvania), 48
civility/rules of civility
    COVID pandemic and, 4–5
    definition of, 9
    differing views on, 8–9
    Donald Trump and, 41–42
    students advocate for, 49–52
    as tool to neutralize opposition, 14
Civil Rights Act (1964), 11
civil society, 9
    impact of Donald Trump's language on, 43
CNN, 26, 30, 31, 35
    reporting on immigration debate by, 33
Colmes, Alan, 30
conspiracy theories, 32, 37
    prevalence of belief in, 35–36
Constitution, US, 14, 24
    social contract and, 9–10
    See also First Amendment
COVID-19 pandemic, 4
    and hostility over mask mandates, 19–21
Crossfire (TV program), 26, 30

Deery, June, 40
Deforest, Ricardo, 37
dopamine, 33–34

Ellis, Renee, 51–52

Facebook, 34–35, 36
FAIR, 33
Fairness Doctrine, 29
Fann, Karen, 45
Federal Aviation Administration (FAA), 21
Federal Bureau of Investigation (FBI), 23
Federal Communications Commission (FCC), 28–29
First Amendment, 14, 49
flight attendants, air rage and, 4, 21
Florida Atlantic University, 31–32
Floyd, George, 13, 41
Fox News, 29–31, 30
    messaging on, 32
    political leanings of viewers of, 31
    reporting on immigration debate by, 33

Garland, Merrick, 24
Gideon, Sara, **54,** 54–55
Guide for Youth Activists (American Civil Liberties Union of Tennessee), 16
Gupta, Edha, 51

Hannity, Sean, 30, 32
Hannity & Colmes (TV program), 30
hate/hate crimes
    anti-Asian, 41–42
    use of term on Fox News versus MSNBC, 32
Haugen, Frances, 34, **35**
Hayes, Jahana, 47
Hobbes, Thomas, 9

iCivics, 56, 61
iHeartMedia, 28
immigration debate, reporting on, 33
Ingraham, Laura, 32
Instagram, 34

JOBS Act (2012), 38
Johnson, Lyndon B., 11
Jones, Robert, 43

Kaiser Family Foundation, 32
Keeping It Civil (podcast), 55
King, Martin Luther, Jr., 10–12, **12**
Klein, Jonathan, 26
Kogan, Vladimir, 22

Laats, Adam, 25
Lauter, David, 46–47
"Letter from a Birmingham Jail" (King), 10–11
Leviathan (Hobbes), 9
LGBTQ rights, 25
Limbaugh, Rush, 28–29, **29**

manners, 15
    civic activism and, 16
mask mandates
    anger over, 21
    protests against, 22, **23**
    support of, 19
McConnell, Mitch, 38–39
McNamara, Mary, 28
Moms for Liberty, 24–25
Morganstein, Joshua, 6, 7
Morris, Kiah, 47
Mosley, Adam, 4, 5
MSNBC, 31
    reporting on immigration debate by, 33
Murdoch, Rupert, 29–30

National Constitution Center, 61
National Institute for Civil Discourse (NICD), 53–54, 61
National School Boards Association (NSBA), 24
New York Times (newspaper), 41
Next Generation program (National Institute for Civil Discourse), 53–54, 56
Norwood, Candice, 47
Novaco, Raymond, 4

Obama, Barack, 38, 39, 46
O'Neil, Luke, 37
opinion polls. *See* surveys

Packer, ZZ, 9–10, 16

Panther Anti-Racist Union (PARU), 50–51
Paris, Katie, 52, **52**
Pew Research Center, 31, 32
politicians
Black female, harassment of, 47
decline in compromise among, 38–39
targeting of, 5, 45–46
training programs to increase civility among, 53–56
polls. *See* surveys
Pouliot, Matt, 56
presidential election, 2020, 32
Public Religion Research Institute, 43

Rachel Maddow Show, The (TV program), 31
Rangel, Isadora, 46
Red Wine & Blue network, 52–53
restaurant workers, assaults against, **18**, 18–19
Rios, Alexis, 17
Rogers, Wendy, 43–45
Rose, Chris, 45
Rules of Civility and Decent Behaviour in Company and Conversation (Washington), 8
Rush Limbaugh Show, The (talk radio show), 28

school board meetings, 22
efforts to de-escalate tensions at, 52–53
Selepak, Andrew, 34
Sellers, Joshua, 55
Sheridan, Brenda, 22, 23
Skitka, Linda, 25
social contract theory, 9
social media, 34–35
link between cable news media and, 36
Stewart, Jon, 26, 27, **27**

surveys
of Democrats/Republicans on views of opposing party, 32, 40
on importance of free speech rights, 49
on level of civility in society, 56
on percentage of Americans having no/few friends of opposite political persuasion, 38
on prevalence of belief in conspiracy theories, 35–36
on prevalence of youth attending BLM marches, 25
on support for political violence, by party, 43
on support of mask mandates, 19
on viewership of cable news, 31

Taibbi, Matt, 30–31, 33
Thomson, Henry, 55
TikTok, 34
Trump, Donald, 32, 37, 46
as rewarded for incivility, 40–41
Twitter page of, **44**
Tucker Carlson Tonight (TV program), 36
Twitter, 35, 41, 43, **44**

University of Pennsylvania, 48
Up to Us, 56
US Department of Justice, 24

Voting Rights Act (1965), 11

Washington, George, 8
Wasow, Omar, 17
Wilson, Joe, 39

Youth Leadership Initiative, 56

Zamalin, Alex, 14, 15
Zuckerberg, Mark, 34